The Second Treatise of the Great Seth

Revealing the Hidden Wisdom of the Savior

A Modern Translation

Adapted for the Contemporary Reader

**Jesus Christ
(Gnostic Tradition)**

Translated by Tim Zengerink

© **Copyright 2025**
All rights reserved.

It is not legal to reproduce, duplicate, or transmit any part of this document in either electronic means or in printed format. Recording of this publication is strictly prohibited and any storage of this document is not allowed unless with written permission from the publisher except for the use of brief quotations in a book review.

This book contains works of fiction. Any resemblance to persons living or dead, or places, events, or locations is purely coincidental.

Table Of Contents

Preface - Message to the Reader 1

Introduction 5

The Second Treatise of The Great Seth 11

Thank You for Reading 30

Preface - Message to the Reader

What If You Could Help Rebuild the Greatest Library in Human History?

Thousands of years ago, the Library of Alexandria stood as the crown jewel of human achievement — a sanctuary where the collected wisdom of every known civilization was gathered, preserved, and shared freely.

And then, it was lost.

Through fire, conquest, and the slow erosion of time, humanity lost not just books — but ideas, dreams, discoveries, and stories that could have changed the world forever.

Today, the Library of Alexandria lives again — and you are invited to be a part of its restoration.

Our mission is simple yet profound:

To rebuild the greatest library the world has ever known, and to translate all timeless works into every language and dialect, so that no seeker of knowledge is ever left behind again.

By joining our movement to rebuild the modern Library of Alexandria, you become part of an unprecedented mission:

- **Unlimited Access to the Greatest Audiobooks & eBooks Ever Written:**

  Instantly explore thousands of legendary works—Plato, Shakespeare, Jane Austen, Leo Tolstoy, and countless more. All instantly available to read or listen, placing a complete literary universe at your fingertips.

- **Beautiful Paperback & Deluxe Editions at Printing Cost**

  Own any title as an elegant paperback, deluxe hardcover, or stunning collectible boxset—offered to you at true printing cost, delivered straight to your door. Build your personal Library of Alexandria, crafted for beauty, built for durability, and worthy of proud display.

- **Fresh Translations for Modern Readers—in Every Language & Dialect**

  Enjoy timeless masterpieces reimagined in clear, contemporary language—no more outdated phrases or obscure references. Alongside the original versions, we're tirelessly translating these classics into every language and dialect imaginable, ensuring accessibility and understanding across cultures and generations.

- **Join a Global Renaissance of Literature & Knowledge**

    You directly support expanding our library, publishing deluxe editions at true cost, translating works into all global languages, and bringing humanity's greatest stories to people everywhere. By joining today, you're not just preserving a legacy of masterpieces; you set in motion a powerful wave of literary accessibility.

Become a Torchbearer of Knowledge.

Join us for free now at **LibraryofAlexandria.com**

Together, we will ensure that the light of human wisdom never fades again.

With gratitude and a shared love of knowledge,

The Modern Library of Alexandria Team

Visit:

www.libraryofalexandria.com

Or scan the code below:

Introduction

The Savior Speaks: A Radical Revelation of Truth

The Second Treatise of the Great Seth is among the most striking and controversial writings preserved within the corpus of Gnostic texts discovered at Nag Hammadi. Attributed to Jesus Christ, this revelatory treatise offers a first-person account from the Savior himself, not in the voice of humility or submission, but as a triumphant and knowing guide. With poetic intensity and theological boldness, it proclaims a profound vision of salvation that diverges sharply from orthodox Christian teachings. Here, the crucifixion is described not as a moment of suffering, but as an illusion—a misunderstanding of the true spiritual mission of the Savior. The result is a dramatic retelling of divine history, one that challenges conventional beliefs and invites readers to awaken to a higher spiritual reality.

At the heart of this text is the idea that the material world is a product of ignorance—a distorted reflection of the true divine realm. The rulers and powers of the world, whom orthodox traditions might identify as legitimate authorities or even divine agents, are here portrayed as arrogant impostors: blind to the truth, enforcers of illusion, and unwitting servants of the Demiurge, the lower creator god. In contrast, the Savior speaks as one who transcends all these powers. He has not come to suffer, but to reveal; not to submit, but to enlighten.

This is not a gospel of blood sacrifice, but of cosmic awakening. The Savior in The Second Treatise of the Great Seth declares that he entered the world invisibly, moving among people without being fully seen, misunderstood by the powers of the age. He mocks those who thought they had captured and crucified him. They crucified a body, he says, but not him. He remained untouched, unbound, and ever free. This claim, while startling, is central to the Gnostic view of salvation. It affirms that true divinity cannot be harmed by material forces, and that liberation comes not through physical death, but through spiritual knowledge—gnosis.

This revelation is not meant to belittle the suffering of others, but to lift the veil of illusion that binds the soul. It tells us that the truth is deeper than appearances, and that what most people worship is not the true God, but a false image shaped by fear, ignorance, and control. The Savior comes to liberate souls from this deception—not by overthrowing governments, but by awakening the divine spark within each person. He speaks with the authority of one who has seen beyond the veil and calls others to do the same.

The use of the name "Seth" in the title is deeply symbolic. In Gnostic cosmology, Seth is the third son of Adam and Eve, but more importantly, he is considered the progenitor of a spiritual lineage—the "immovable race"—who retain the divine light within them. The Savior in this text aligns himself with that race, declaring solidarity with those who have been rejected, mocked, and marginalized by the world. He is not ashamed of the truth; he is ashamed only of the lies and pretensions of those who wield false authority. This inversion of values is a hallmark of Gnostic teaching: what the world despises, God honors; what the world praises, God often rejects.

The Illusion of the World and the Victory of Spirit

A central theme in The Second Treatise of the Great Seth is the distinction between reality and illusion. The material world, with its systems of control, religious hierarchies, and violent power structures, is portrayed not as the work of the true God, but as a counterfeit realm governed by arrogant rulers. These rulers—called archons in other Gnostic texts—enforce conformity, suppress knowledge, and persecute the enlightened. They are blind guides, leading others into deeper blindness.

In response, the Savior does not fight them on their terms. Instead, he reveals their ignorance by refusing to be captured by their illusion. His "crucifixion" is a moment of divine irony—an event in which the powers believe they have triumphed, but in fact only expose their own blindness. He allows the illusion to play out while remaining entirely untouched in spirit. His victory is not one of physical might or worldly acclaim, but of transcendent truth. He cannot be harmed because he does not belong to their world. His kingdom is not of this earth—but of light, spirit, and truth.

This radical reimagining of the crucifixion has profound implications for how we understand suffering, salvation, and spiritual identity. Rather than viewing the Passion as the fulfillment of a blood-based atonement system, The Second Treatise of the Great Seth invites us to see it as the moment when illusion was exposed and truth revealed. The Savior does not die to satisfy a vengeful deity—he comes to shatter the illusion that binds the soul and to model the path of spiritual liberation.

The reader is therefore called not to worship the image of the crucified man, but to follow the example of the free spirit. To walk the path of truth is to see through the masks of religion, politics, and social convention. It is to recognize that the world's values are often inverted—that the humble are truly exalted, that the poor in spirit are closest to the divine, that the kingdom of light lies not in the heavens above, but within. The Savior's message is one of radical freedom. Nothing can bind the awakened soul—not law, not death, not even the cross.

This perspective also recasts the role of scripture, authority, and tradition. The Second Treatise of the Great Seth does not depend on external institutions to validate its truth. It speaks directly to the reader's own divine intuition, calling forth the remembrance of a truth already known, if only dimly. It encourages the reader to trust the inner voice, to question inherited doctrines, and to embrace the solitary path of gnosis. This is not a comfortable journey—it is a revolutionary one. But it is the only path that leads to genuine freedom.

This modern translation has been prepared with care to retain the poetic strength, spiritual depth, and prophetic tone of the original. Archaic language has been refined, dense metaphors clarified, and complex cosmological references made more accessible—without sacrificing the intensity of the original message. The result is a version of The Second Treatise of the

Great Seth that invites the reader into a living dialogue with the divine. It is not a static text; it is a spiritual transmission.

To read this treatise is to encounter a Savior who defies all expectations. He does not demand worship—he demands awakening. He does not ask for belief—he calls for remembrance. He does not point outward—he turns us inward, toward the truth that has never left us.

Let these words be your guide into the sacred mystery. Let them challenge your assumptions, dismantle your illusions, and awaken your inner knowing. For in these pages, you will find not only the voice of the Savior, but the echo of your own soul's longing for truth, freedom, and divine light.

The Second Treatise of The Great Seth

The perfect Majesty lives forever in a place of endless peace, surrounded by the pure light that comes from the mother of all things. Everyone who comes to me and is joined with me becomes complete, because I am made perfect through the Word. I exist in harmony with the full greatness of the Spirit, which is not just a companion to us but also part of our very being. This Spirit gave birth to a glorious Word, revealing the goodness of our Father. Within this Word is a thought that never fades—a pure, sacred truth that is beyond understanding, flowing like divine waters. I live within you, and you live within me, just as the Father exists in you in pure innocence.

Let us come together as one. Let us go out and bring light to creation. Let us send a messenger to those places, just as the Father once visited the Ennoias, descending into the lower realms. I spoke these words before the great gathering of Majesty, and the entire house of the Father of Truth rejoiced, celebrating that I came from among them. From the pure Spirit, I formed a thought about the Ennoias and their descent into the lower waters. Everyone in the assembly had the same purpose, united in spirit and truth. Seeing that I was willing, they entrusted me with this mission. I came forward to reveal the Father's glory to my kin and my fellow spirits.

Those who lived in the world had already been prepared by our sister Sophia. Though her work had flaws, her intentions were pure, even if unspoken and unnoticed. She did not seek help or guidance from the whole assembly, the greatness of the divine, or the fullness of the Pleroma. Acting alone, she prepared places for the Son of Light and his companions. She used the elements of the lower realms to shape bodies for them. But these bodies, made with a temporary and hollow glory, could not last forever. Their weakness reflected the imperfection of their origins because they were formed only by Sophia's hand.

Now, they wait, ready to receive the life-giving Word from the eternal One. They wait for the greatness of those who stand firm in the truth. Through the Word, and through those who remain faithful in me, they will be renewed and restored, realigned with the eternal light. Together, those who endure will bring glory to the Father and his everlasting Majesty.

I entered a physical body, removing the one who had lived in it before. I took my place within it, and when I did, the rulers of the world were thrown into confusion. All the material things under their control, along with the powers of the earth, trembled when they saw the Image within me, for it was unlike anything they had ever known. The body they had controlled before was earthly and limited, but now I was inside it—coming from above the heavens, carrying within me the eternal and divine essence.

Even though I did not refuse to be the Christ, I kept my full identity and love hidden from them. Instead, I made it clear that I was not from their lower, earthly world. This caused the entire material realm to be thrown into chaos. Confusion spread everywhere, and the rulers' plans began to fall apart. Many were amazed and shaken by the miracles I performed. Some, feeling drawn to the truth, chose to believe and escaped along with those who had come down with me. They ran in fear from the one who had abandoned the throne and instead turned to Sophia, the source of hope, who had warned them of my coming and the gathering of those with me—the true people of Adonaios.

Others, however, fled as if they were running from the great ruler of the world and his followers, who had brought every kind of suffering upon me. They were overwhelmed, struggling to decide what to do about me. In their confusion, they failed to understand the greatness of Sophia, and they spoke falsely about the Man and the true assembly of light. Their ignorance and blindness became clear because they could not recognize the Father of Truth or the Man of Greatness. Instead, they held onto false ideas they had created out of their lack of understanding. They had built a false foundation, one meant to hide their own corruption. In their foolishness, they even tried to destroy Adam, the being they themselves had made, hoping that by doing so, they could keep their control hidden.

The rulers, especially those serving Yaldabaoth, worked hard to cover up the truth about the realm of angels, trying to prevent humanity from discovering the true Man. But Adam, the one they had created, stood right before them as a reminder of what they could not understand. A great fear spread through their entire kingdom because the angels who surrounded them were beginning to question everything. Without those who offered true praise, the rulers feared their archangel would become powerless and empty.

Then, in arrogance, the ruler of the world declared to his angels, "I am God, and there is no one besides me." But I laughed, knowing how empty his claim was. He asked, "Who is this Man?" At the same time, his angels, having seen Adam and the dwelling prepared for him, mocked and insulted him. Their own thoughts and purpose had become weak, disconnected from the true Majesty of the heavens. They could not recognize the true Man because they were trapped in their own ignorance.

As the angels laughed at Adam, thinking him small and unimportant, they unknowingly revealed their own emptiness. Their so-called wisdom was actually blindness, and they failed to see the greatness hidden in the true Man, whom they dismissed as insignificant. In their foolishness, they did not recognize the light that would eventually expose their vanity and ignorance, nor did they understand the power that was beyond their reach.

The complete greatness of the Spirit's Fatherhood remained in its eternal place, untouched and at peace. I have been with Him from the very beginning, holding within me the purpose and knowledge of a single, eternal truth—one that comes from the pure and boundless mysteries beyond human understanding. I placed this small but powerful thought into the world, disrupting the rulers' order and filling them with fear. My presence brought fire and light, shaking everything connected to them, because my thought, my purpose, caused all these events to unfold.

A great disturbance rose among them. The Seraphim and Cherubim, whose glory was fading, found themselves caught in conflict. Confusion spread across the realm of Adonaios and his dwelling, reaching even to the great ruler of the world and those who conspired against me. Some said, "Let's capture him," while others hesitated, fearing their plan would fail.

Adonaios recognized me because he held onto hope. I stood among fierce enemies, but I did not fall into their trap. Their plan, created out of ignorance and foolishness, was meant to capture me, but I did not give in. They tried to harm me, but I was never truly affected. Even though they believed they had made me suffer, I did not truly die—it only appeared that way. This was necessary to protect myself from disgrace, even as I stood among my own people. I removed the shame they tried to place upon me and remained strong, refusing to give in to fear or the suffering they tried to force upon me.

I went through suffering as they believed it to be, making sure they could never truly understand what had happened. The death they thought they inflicted on me was actually their own, caused by their mistakes and blindness. They nailed a man to the cross, thinking they were crucifying me, but they never really saw me. They were blind and deaf to my presence, and in their actions, they condemned themselves. They believed they had punished me, but it was actually their own ruler who tasted the bitterness of gall and vinegar. It was not me they struck with the reed or made carry the cross—that was Simon. The crown of thorns was placed on another, not on me. Meanwhile, I was above, rejoicing, watching the rulers and the results of their ignorance. I laughed at how little they understood.

I overcame all their powers. As I moved among them, no one recognized me for who I truly was. I changed my appearance, taking on different forms as needed. When I came to their gates, I looked like them and passed unnoticed. I walked freely in their spaces, without fear or shame, because I remained untouched by their corruption. I spoke with them, moving among them through those who were mine. I stood up against those who mistreated my own, putting out the fire of their hatred.

I did all of this with a firm purpose—to carry out the will of the Father above. The Son of the Majesty, who had been hidden in the lower realms, was lifted up to the heights, where I remained with him in the eternal places. These heights cannot be seen or known by those outside, for they are part of the unspoiled, everlasting bridal chamber. Unlike the world that fades and decays, this chamber is new, whole, and beyond the reach of destruction. It cannot be divided or fully described in words. It is universal, eternal, and complete.

A soul that comes from the heights does not focus on the failures of this world or remain trapped in the lower realms. When the soul is freed and made noble, it will stand before the Father without fear or exhaustion, forever joined with the divine mind and power. Those who see me will recognize themselves in me and become one with me. They will enter without fear, passing through every barrier, and will reach the highest glory, where truth is revealed, and all is made whole.

During my return to the revealed heights—an event the world refused to believe—I experienced my third baptism, appearing in a form they could perceive. When the seven rulers of fire were scattered, and the false sun that powered the archons was put out, darkness fell upon them. The world became weak, trapped in chains of ignorance and confusion. They nailed the one they did not understand to a tree, fastening him with four brass nails. But in their blindness, they missed the greater truth. He tore the temple veil with his own hands, and the earth trembled in chaos. That shaking freed the souls that had been trapped in a state of sleep, releasing them from ignorance and death. They rose up boldly, no longer stuck in blind servitude. They cast off their old selves and put on a new identity, having found the true Blessed One—the eternal, unknowable Father, the endless light that I am.

I returned to my own and brought them into unity with me, a reunion that needed no long explanation, because our thoughts and understanding were already one. They understood me instantly because we shared the same essence and purpose. Together, we decided to bring an end to the rulers, following the will of the Father, who is one with me.

When we left our home above and entered this world, we were rejected and mistreated. This opposition didn't just come from those who were ignorant but also from those who claimed to follow Christ. Yet, they acted without understanding, their emptiness keeping them blind to the truth about themselves. Like thoughtless creatures, they attacked the very people I had freed, hating those who carried my message. Their hatred came from their inability to truly understand me. They served not just one master, but many, divided in their loyalty. But you will overcome all these struggles—conflicts, jealousy, and anger. Through the purity of our love, you will remain innocent, good, and connected to the Father, who holds the great mystery of our existence.

This world, lost in ignorance, acted foolishly. I saw its confusion, for the rulers could not comprehend the deep connection shared by the sons of light. In their misunderstanding, they tried to imitate this divine unity by creating a false teaching based on a dead man and deception. They attempted to copy the purity and freedom of the true gathering but instead built their beliefs around fear, control, and earthly concerns. Their rituals were empty, revealing their smallness and ignorance. Lacking the nobility of truth, they rejected the one who lived within them and worshiped something outside of themselves, completely blind to the wisdom and greatness of the truth that comes from above.

True knowledge does not come from fear, jealousy, or attachment to material things. Those who possess the truth use what they have freely, knowing it comes from a higher source. They are not ruled by desire, for their authority comes from within—a law they carry in their own hearts. But those without truth are empty, always craving what they lack. Their desire leads them to mislead others, trapping them in servitude and fear. They mistake control for divine will, forcing others into ignorance. But the Father's greatness is not found in such force. He protects only those who belong to him—those who live in harmony with his will, free from oppression, and aligned with his true purpose. In this unity, those who are perfect remain beyond words, whole, and a living testimony to the divine.

The perfect ones are meant to be established in this way, united with me in wisdom—not just by hearing words, but through action. In their unity, they do not fight against each other but share in true friendship. Through the Good One, I complete all things, for true unity leaves no room for division. Those who stir up conflict will learn nothing, as they isolate themselves and create hostility. But those who live in harmony, embracing brotherly love sincerely and without favoritism, embody the true desire of the Father. They are whole, complete, and the perfect reflection of love. This is the true union—one of peace, harmony, and the fulfillment of the Father's eternal will.

Adam became a mockery because the rulers who created him tried to make him a substitute for true humanity, claiming he was greater than me and my brothers. Yet we remain innocent, for we have done nothing wrong. Abraham, Isaac, and Jacob were also used as imitations of true patriarchs, as if they could be placed above me and my brothers. Still, we remain free of guilt, for we have not sinned.

David, too, was made into an object of deception when they declared his son to be the Son of Man, as if this could make him greater than me and my kindred. Yet we are without blame, for we have done no wrong. Solomon, filled with pride, was also deceived. He believed himself to be the Christ, tricked by the rulers who convinced him he could surpass me and my brothers. But we remain innocent, for we have not sinned.

Even the twelve prophets became part of this deception, appearing as mere shadows of the true prophets. These false figures were created by the rulers, as if they could overshadow me and my brothers. Yet, we remain without blame, for we have done nothing wrong.

Moses, though praised as a faithful servant and "the Friend," became a symbol of misunderstanding. They told false stories about him, for he never truly knew me. Neither he nor anyone before him—from Adam to Moses to John the Baptist—ever knew me or my brothers. Their teachings, focused on angels, strict rules about food, and a life of servitude, were built on error. They had no real understanding of the truth and were blinded by a great deception that kept them from finding freedom in true wisdom. Because of this blindness, they could never truly understand until they came to know the Son of Man.

Regarding my Father, I am the one the world failed to understand. Because of this ignorance, the world turned against me and my brothers. But even though they opposed us, we remain innocent. We have not done wrong. Their failure was not just about not knowing me—it was about not recognizing the truth itself. The rulers of this world blinded them, trapping them in deception and leading them into a life of fear and false beliefs. They trust in illusions instead of reality. Until they come to know the Son of Man, they will continue down the wrong path, holding on to lies. But while they stumble, we remain free from their mistakes, for we have not given in to falsehood.

The false ruler became a joke when he proudly declared, "I am God, and there is no one greater than me. I alone am the Father and Lord, and no one exists beside me. I am a jealous God, punishing the children for the sins of their fathers for three and four generations." He spoke as if his power was above mine and my brothers'. But even with all his boasting, we remain innocent, for we have not sinned. We have seen through his false teachings and empty pride. He does not belong to our true Father, nor does he reflect the truth of the divine. His words, full of arrogance and self-importance, stand in complete contrast to the greatness of the eternal Father.

In his pride, he showed himself as a fool, offering nothing but judgments built on lies and prophecies filled with deception. His words carried the weight of ignorance, but through our unity and understanding, we saw the truth behind his empty claims. He spoke and acted from a place of darkness, unable to grasp the reality of the true Father and the infinite wisdom of the divine.

And to those who are blind, you don't even realize how deep your blindness goes. Your lack of understanding has been with you for ages, and it has never been lifted. You are trapped in your ignorance, unwilling to listen to the truth. Because of this, you have fallen into error, misled by lies. In your blindness, you have raised your hands in violence against what you do not understand, as if you were swinging at the air, accomplishing nothing but feeding your own foolishness.

Those who refuse to see remain trapped, locked in chains of their own making. They are slaves to the law and the fear of earthly things, unable to rise above their limited understanding. They hold onto rules and illusions, believing these will save them, when in reality, they only keep them far from the truth. The more they cling to falsehood, the deeper their ignorance becomes. They cannot see the light or escape the darkness they have created for themselves. Their devotion to fear and deception keeps them from finding the freedom and knowledge that the true Father offers.

I am Christ, the Son of Man, the one who has come from among you and walks beside you. I am rejected for your sake so that you can rise above division and see unity instead of separation. Do not fall into the trap of becoming like those who give birth to evil, for this will lead to jealousy, division, anger, hatred, fear, doubt, and empty desires. But know this: I am a mystery beyond words, a truth that cannot be fully grasped, yet one that calls you to seek and grow.

Before the world was created, when the entire heavenly Assembly gathered in the sacred places above, they made a plan for a union—a wedding that is not of the physical world but a spiritual joining of all things in perfect harmony. In these pure and untouched realms, this union was completed through a living Word. This perfect wedding took place through Jesus, the one who connects everything and holds all things together. He is the expression of undivided love and the eternal power that brings unity.

Though he is surrounded by all, he remains one—existing beyond all limits, holding all thoughts and all life within him. He stands as both a father and a source of life, for he came from the Father, who is the fountain of perfect truth. From this highest and purest place comes eternal life, a peace beyond understanding, and a joy that is whole and unshaken. This joy is eternal and unites all things in faith, love, wisdom, and truth.

This sacred Assembly, in its wisdom, is connected to the divine understanding that reaches into all things with joy and faithfulness, always remaining steady and attentive. This understanding, or Nous, exists in the roles of father, mother, and brother, working together with wisdom as the foundation of all truth. This union is like a perfect marriage, a place where the spirit of truth dwells, shining a light that cannot be described, a mystery beyond words.

This unity cannot exist in division, conflict, or unrest. It thrives only in peace and harmony, where love brings everything together. It is a perfection that is greater than any single place or time, completed in the one who is eternal and whole. It is a truth that calls us beyond separation, inviting us into oneness, where love and unity are the ultimate reality. In this state, everything is perfected in the presence of the divine.

This truth was also revealed in the lower realms, bringing reconciliation. Those who recognized me as salvation, and those who lived for the glory of the Father and truth, were brought together as one through the living Word. I am present in the spirit and truth of the divine Mother, just as I have always been. I walked among those who are bound together in eternal friendship—a friendship without hostility, without evil, rooted in unity through the knowledge I have shared. This peace is perfect, existing within and among them, and it spreads endlessly.

Those who have taken on my likeness will also take on my Word. These are the ones who will step into the light forever, joined in eternal friendship through the Spirit. They will come to know, with complete certainty and without doubt, that all things are One. And when they recognize this truth, they will become one with it, just as the Assembly and all who dwell within it have come to understand. For the Father of all, who is limitless and unchanging, exists as understanding, speech, separation, envy, and fire. Yet he is fully one, containing all things within himself, joined together in perfect unity because they all come from the same Spirit.

To those who do not see—why have you failed to recognize the full mystery? The Father, who has no limits and never changes, is the source of everything. All things flow from his Spirit, and all things return to unity through his Word. The Assembly knows this, and because of this knowledge, they remain in perfect peace, living in harmony with the One.

Those who are joined in the Spirit will be forever united in the light, their bond stronger than any division, their friendship unshaken. They have seen the truth, and by seeing, they have embraced oneness. They have learned its nature and now live in its unity. The greatness of the Father holds all things—even those that seem divided or in conflict—within his infinite oneness. This is a lesson for those who seek wisdom and an invitation for those who wish to join the Assembly of eternal light. It is the greatest mystery, the truth that brings all creation together into one unbroken whole.

But the rulers around Yaldabaoth acted in disobedience because of the thoughts that descended to him from his sister, Sophia. They tried to create their own kind of union with those around them, forming it from a fiery cloud born from their jealousy. This mixture led to the creation of others among them, as if they could damage or destroy the joy and harmony of the higher Assembly. Their actions created chaos and confusion, forming a false mixture of fire, earth, and even a violent nature. They were limited, small in spirit, unwise, and lacked understanding, yet they tried to accomplish things they did not comprehend. They did not realize that light belongs with light, darkness belongs with darkness, the corruptible joins with what will perish, and the eternal remains with the incorruptible.

I share these truths with you now, for I am Jesus Christ, the Son of Man, lifted above the heavens, beyond the reach of corruption. I reveal these things to you, the perfect and incorruptible ones, because of the pure and eternal mystery—the unspoken truth that holds everything together in harmony. The rulers, trapped in their delusions, mistakenly believe that we gave them power before the foundation of the world. They do not understand that when we rise from the world's domains, we carry with us the signs of incorruption—a spiritual union born from knowledge and truth.

You don't see the truth because your physical body hides it from you. It blocks your vision and keeps you from understanding. But I alone am a true companion of wisdom. From the very beginning, I have been with the Father, living in the place of truth and endless greatness. This has always been my home, and I invite you, my kindred spirits and brothers, to join me here and find peace.

Come now, because you do not belong to this temporary world. You come from a light that never fades, from a truth that can never be broken. Hold on to this knowledge and to the unity we share. Our connection is eternal, not built on things that disappear, but on the lasting mysteries of the Father—the source of all that is pure and unchanging. We will always be together, joined in spirit and truth, because that is the nature of those called to a place of perfection. So rest with me in the endless joy and peace of what cannot be broken, where we will live in the light forever.

Thank You for Reading

Dear Reader,

We hope this timeless classic has sparked your imagination and enriched your literary journey. Now that you've turned the final page, we want to share a vision for the future of reading—one where every classic you've ever wanted to explore is at your fingertips, in a format that best suits your life.

We'd like to invite you to gain immediate, unlimited digital & audiobook access to hundreds of the most treasured literary classics ever written—along with the option to secure deluxe paperback, hardcover & box set editions at printing cost. Together, we can spark a new global literary renaissance alongside our small, independent publishing house called "The Library of Alexandria."

Thousands of years ago, the Library of Alexandria stood as a beacon of knowledge—until it was lost to history. We aim to reignite that spirit of preservation and discovery right now, in the modern age—only this time, it's accessible to all, in every language and every format.

Picture a world where every timeless classic, novel, poem, or philosophical treatise is not only available to read but also updated for today's readers—modernized, translated into any language or dialect, and ready to enjoy in any format you choose, whether that is in an eBook, audiobook, paperback, or deluxe hardcover & box set version a printing cost.

By joining our movement to rebuild the modern Library of Alexandria, you become part of an unprecedented mission to offer:

- **Unlimited Audiobook & eBook Access to the Greatest Classics of All Time**

  Instantly explore thousands of legendary works, from Plato and Shakespeare to Jane Austen and Leo Tolstoy. All are instantly ready to read or listen to, giving you a complete literary universe at your fingertips.

- **Paperback & Deluxe Editions at Printing Costs:**

  Purchase any title in a paperback, deluxe hardbound, or deluxe boxset edition at printing costs, shipped right to your doorstep. Curate your personal library of Alexandria with editions worthy of display—crafted to last, designed to captivate, and delivered straight to your door.

- **Modern translations for Contemporary Readers in all languages and dialects**

  Discover a vast selection of classics reimagined in clear, current language—no more struggling with outdated phrases or obscure references. Next to the original versions, we aim to offer translations in as many languages and dialects as possible.

  As we continue our translation efforts and add new languages, readers everywhere can connect with these works as if they were written today. By bridging linguistic divides, you're contributing to ensuring that these timeless stories become more meaningful, accessible, and inspiring for people across the globe.

- **Your Personal Library of Alexandria:**

  Over the months and years, you'll curate a unique physical archive of classics—each volume a testament to your taste, curiosity, and love of knowledge. It's not just about owning books—it's about curating a cultural legacy you'll cherish and pass down for generations to come.

- **Join a Global Literary Renaissance:**

  Your support fuels an ongoing mission: allowing us to reinvest in offering deluxe print editions (including special boxsets) at their true cost, broaden the range of available formats and translations, and extend the reach of these works to new audiences worldwide. By joining today, you're not just preserving a legacy of masterpieces; you set in motion a powerful wave of literary accessibility.

We are more than a publisher—we're a movement, and we can't do it alone. Your support lets us scale our mission, preserving and reimagining history's greatest works for tomorrow's readers.

Become a Torchbearer of knowledge.

Thank you for picking up this book and allowing us into your literary journey. As you turn the pages, know that you're part of something larger: a global effort to keep these stories alive, share their wisdom across borders and generations, and spark a true cultural revival for the modern era.

If this resonates with you—please consider taking the next step by visiting:

www.libraryofalexandria.com

With gratitude and a shared love of knowledge,

The Modern Library of Alexandria Team

Visit:

www.libraryofalexandria.com

Or scan the code below:

www.ingramcontent.com/pod-product-compliance
Lightning Source LLC
LaVergne TN
LVHW030631080426
835512LV00021B/3461